DATE DUE

DEC - 3 2002			
JAN - 7 2004			

DEMCO 38-297

Marco Polo
and the Wonders of the East

Marco Polo
and the Wonders of the East

Hal Marcovitz

Chelsea House Publishers
Philadelphia

Prepared for Chelsea House Publishers by:
OTTN Publishing, Warminster, PA

CHELSEA HOUSE PUBLISHERS
Editor in Chief: Stephen Reginald
Managing Editor: James D. Gallagher
Production Manager: Pamela Loos
Art Director: Sara Davis
Director of Photography: Judy L. Hasday
Senior Production Editor: LeeAnne Gelletly
Series Designer: Keith Trego

3 5 7 9 8 6 4

Library of Congress Cataloging-in-Publication Data

Marcovitz, Hal.
   Marco Polo / by Hal Marcovitz
p.   cm. – (Explorers of new worlds)
Includes bibliographical references and index.
Summary: A biography of the Italian traveler who
became the first European to cross Asia completely
and document his experiences.
ISBN 0-7910-5511-6
1. Polo, Marco, 1254–1323? Juvenile literature.
2. Travelers–Italy Biography Juvenile literature.
 [1. Polo, Marco, 1254–1323? 2. Explorers. 3. Voyages
and travels 4. Asia–Description and travel.] I. Title.
II. Series.
G370.P9M37   1999
915.04'2'0925–dc21   99-22255
                                                  CIP

Contents

"This Book Will
Be a Truthful
One"

Explorers of New Worlds

This painting shows what the busy harbor of Venice looked like in Marco Polo's day. Venice was an important city in Italy, on the coast of the Mediterranean Sea.

I

A s the sun dipped low in the west on the afternoon of September 6, 1296, two powerful
navies came within sight of one another and made ready
for battle. One fleet of warships was fighting for Genoa,
the other for Venice. Venice and Genoa were **city-states—**
powerful cities in Italy that controlled all the territory
around them. The ships would be fighting for control of
trade on the Mediterranean Sea.

The sailors of Venice and Genoa fought their sea battle in galleys like this one—long ships that used sails and oars to maneuver on the Mediterranean Sea.

Genoa sent 75 ships to the battle under the command of Lamba Doria, a battle-hardened admiral. Doria's ships gathered near Curzola Island in the Mediterranean Sea, near present-day Yugoslavia. Venice countered with a larger **armada**—96 ships under the leadership of Admiral Andrea Dandolo.

One of the ships in the Venetian navy was commanded by a man named Marco Polo. He was a well-to-do explorer and merchant who had only recently returned to his home in Venice. Marco had spent the previous 24 years exploring China and other lands of the Far East. He was a friend of Kublai Khan, the ruler of the powerful Mongol Empire. Now, he was preparing to fight for Venice.

Because of Marco Polo's wealth and his family's place in the city's society, he had been given command of one of the Venetian ships. The battle would be fought by **galleys**: great wooden vessels that could be rowed with oars or powered by the wind.

In the 13th century, naval battles were fierce and bloody conflicts. The sailors would maneuver the galley close to an enemy's ship. Bowmen would shoot arrows at the sailors on the other galley, and lancers would hurl their spears at the enemy. The captain of the galley might also attempt to ram the enemy ship and damage or sink it. Finally, with the enemy's vessel disabled and its crew shaken by the onslaught, soldiers aboard the attacking galley would board the other ship. Then, there would be hand-to-hand fighting until either the crew was killed or captured, or the attackers retreated.

Marco Polo and his family put a lot of their own money into the galley. They outfitted it with 120 oars, two large sails, and even a **catapult** that could hurl stones at the enemy.

Early in the morning of September 7, 1296, the battle started. The men from Venice had more ships, and the wind was in their favor. Soon they captured 10 Genoese galleys. But Lamba Doria's military **prowess** kept the fleet from Genoa from being overmatched. Doria used flags and trumpet calls to signal the captains under his command. Following his orders, the Genoese's galleys continually outmaneuvered the ships of Venice. As the battle continued into late afternoon, 16 more Genoese galleys arrived. These reinforcements helped turn the battle in favor of Genoa.

As the sun sank into the Mediterranean, the Genoese were clearly the victors. A few Venetian galleys managed to escape and carry the news of the defeat back to their home port, but most of the ships from Venice had either been sunk or captured. That night, on the beaches of Curzola, Lamba Doria burned 66 of the captured galleys.

More than 7,000 of the Venetian sailors were killed in the battle. Another 7,400 were taken prisoner. One of the captured sailors was Marco Polo. He was led in chains to a prison in Genoa.

Marco would spend a year in the prison, but it would not be a wasted year. For in prison, he met a writer named Rustichello. The writer had lived in another Italian city-state, Pisa. He had made a living by translating French stories into Italian. The two men became friends.

During their long days and nights sharing a prison cell, Marco told Rustichello about his travels. "What a pity you do not write down all these things, for otherwise they would be lost to the world," Rustichello said to Marco after each story. "No man has ever before seen such wonders!"

"But who would believe me?" Marco answered. "If I recorded the truth I would only be branded a liar!"

But Rustichello would press his friend. "The truth in the end must win out over falsehood," he told Marco.

One day, Marco told Rustichello that he had, in fact, made notes of his travels. He had recorded things he had seen along the **Silk Road**–the network of roads and trails that linked Europe with the East. And he had written about his experiences in the court of the great Kublai Khan. Unfortunately, the notes were at Marco's home in Venice. They were too precious to risk losing at sea while he fought in the war against Genoa.

Rustichello wrote to Marco's father, asking him to send the notes to the prison in Genoa. He bribed one of the guards with a gold piece so that his letter would find its way out of the prison and across Italy to Venice. Weeks later, the guard unlocked the cell door and handed Marco Polo a package. Inside were his precious notes.

Rustichello had some *parchment*—a rough type of paper made from animal skins. He also had goose feathers (he could sharpen these to use as pens) and ink. He told Marco to dictate his story. Rustichello would write it down.

Marco began the book this way: "Ye Emperors, Kings, Dukes, Marquises, Earls, and Knights, and all other people desirous of knowing the diversities of the races of mankind, as well as the diversities of kingdoms, provinces, and regions of all parts of the East, read this book, and ye will find in it the greatest and most marvelous characteristics of the peoples especially of Armenia, Persia, India, and Tartary, as they are severally related in the present work of Marco Polo, a wise and learned citizen of Venice, who states distinctly what things he saw and what things he heard from others. For this book will be a truthful one."

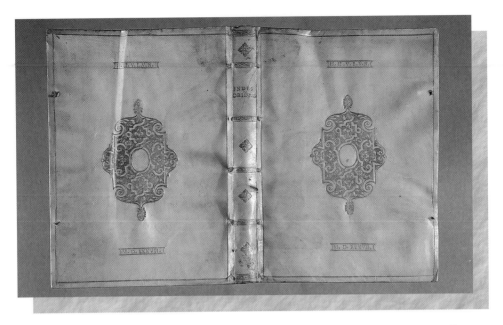

This is the ornate cover of one of the oldest copies of Marco Polo's book A Description of the World. *Marco's tales about his travels would one day be an inspiration to explorers such as Christopher Columbus.*

As Marco spoke this prologue, Rustichello wrote down every word.

And so, for the rest of that year, Marco Polo told the story of his 24-year journey through the East, and Rustichello wrote it down. The book the two men produced would at first be called *A Description of the World.* Eventually, the title of the book would be changed to *The Travels of Marco Polo.* Marco and Rustichello had no way of knowing that the book would one day be an inspiration to many explorers.

The activity of a busy marketplace is captured in this medieval painting. Not much is known about Marco Polo's early life, but members of his family were merchants, so Marco probably was very familiar with settings like this one.

Silk and the Mongol Empire 2

iccolò and Maffeo Polo were brothers in a wealthy Venetian family. They were merchants by trade. The Polos traveled throughout Europe, trading gold, silver, ivory, and gems for such valuable items as furs, ceramic statues and pottery, jade carvings, and bronze or iron objects.

In 1254, Niccolò Polo's son Marco was born. Niccolò would hardly get to know the boy. Soon after Marco's birth, the brothers left on a trading mission to the city of Constantinople. In the 13th century, Constantinople was an important center of culture and trade. (Today, this city is known as Istanbul, and it can be found in Turkey, which is in the Middle East.)

Niccolò and Maffeo remained in Constantinople for six years. In 1260, word reached the brothers that a new emperor had taken power in Cathay (the name by which China was known). His name was Kublai Khan. He was the grandson of the fierce Mongol warrior Genghis Khan, whose armies had conquered a vast area of Asia.

Genghis Khan's empire included modern-day Mongolia, China, Russia, and Iran, and his Mongol warriors might have ridden further west into Europe had Genghis not died suddenly in 1227. Still, by the time Kublai Khan came to the throne, the Mongol Empire remained as powerful and rich as it had been when his grandfather ruled.

Kublai Khan wanted his empire to be at peace. This would allow his merchants to trade with the nations of Western Europe. The Polo brothers were eager to take part in trade with Cathay. They took a cargo of gems eastward, riding on horseback into Mongol lands.

Eventually, the Polos met *emissaries* from Kublai Khan. These messengers asked if the Polos would consider traveling farther east to visit with the emperor. Kublai Khan was always anxious to meet Europeans and learn their ways, they explained.

Yes, the Polos said, they would. And so they made the trek to the city of Shandu, where the Khan kept his summer *palace*. (Today, that city is known as Beijing. It is the capital of modern China.) Kublai Khan showed great hospitality to Niccolò and Maffeo. They stayed in Shandu for nearly nine years.

Eventually, the Polos expressed a desire to return to Venice. Kublai allowed them to leave, but he made the brothers promise they would return. He also asked them to deliver a letter that he had written to Pope Clement IV. In his letter, Kublai asked the pope to send 100 educated Christian men to Cathay. He wanted to learn more about Christianity.

Fifteen years after leaving Venice, Niccolò and Maffeo Polo returned to their home. Niccolò found that his wife had died and that his son Marco was now a teenager. The Polos also

When the Polos left Shandu, Kublai Khan gave them a gold tablet that guaranteed their safe passage through all Mongol lands. An attack on the person who carried the Khan's gold tablet would be regarded as seriously as a crime against the ruler himself!

learned that there was no pope to read Kublai Khan's letter. Pope Clement IV was dead and the Catholic church had yet to name a new pope.

The Polos were eager to return to Cathay, but they did not want to do so without first delivering the Khan's letter to the new pope. They waited for two years, but still a church leader was not chosen. Finally, the Polos decided to lead a new trade mission to Cathay. They could wait no longer. There were riches to be made on the new trade routes opening to the Orient. Also, they feared angering Kublai Khan by delaying their return. So they set off at the head of a caravan.

This time, young Marco would not be left behind. He was 17 years old and anxious to join his father and uncle in their adventures. Niccolò Polo was pleased with the way his son had grown to near-manhood. He decided that Marco was ready to make the trip.

The caravan had only just started when messengers caught up with the

While the older Polos had been away, Marco had prepared to be a merchant. He studied history, arithmetic, and geography, and learned how to speak Persian and how to sail.

Polos and informed them that a new pope, Gregory X, had been elected. They hurried back to Italy, where they met with Pope Gregory X. They gave him the letter from the Khan.

After he read the letter, the new pope wanted to fulfill Kublai Khan's wishes and send 100 Christian clergymen to Cathay. However, he could find only two monks willing to make the long and dangerous trip. Friar Nicolas of Vicenza and Friar William of Tripoli joined the caravan of the Polos, and they started for Cathay.

The Polos would take the Silk Road to Cathay. The Silk Road was not a particular road or caravan trail, but was the name given to several routes that linked Europe and the Far East. Also, the Silk Road was not just a trade route that existed solely for the purpose of trading in *silk*—the soft and elegant fabric that was used to make the clothes worn by the wealthiest people of the 13th century. At the time the Polos were making their way to Cathay, all sorts of goods were being carried along the Silk Road.

The items that were traded ranged from gold and ivory to exotic animals and plants. *Spices* were bought and sold along the Silk Road. From Java, merchants would carry nutmeg; from India, ginger

Silkmakers sort the coocoons of the silkworm in this
image from a 19th century Chinese book on silkmaking.
Because the fine fabric was very valuable, the secrets of
silkmaking were carefully guarded

and cinnamon; from Tibet, traders would deal in
musk. Jewels were also carried back and forth—
diamonds from Golconda, rubies from Badakshan,
turquoise from Yedz, pearls from Ceylon. From
Cathay, merchants would trade porcelain.

Still, of all the precious goods crossing this area, silk—woven from threads produced by tiny silk worms for their cocoons—was the most desired by the people of the West and that is perhaps why the route became known as the Silk Road.

It is often thought that the Romans first encountered silk in one of their wars against the Parthians in what is now Iran in 53 B.C. The Romans obtained samples of this new material, and it quickly became very popular in Rome for its soft texture and elegance. They knew the silk had not been produced by the Parthians. They learned from prisoners that it came from a mysterious tribe in the east, whom the Romans called the "silk people."

The silk people were, in fact, the Chinese, who helped create myths about the fabric in order to preserve their monopoly on its trade. Chinese rulers established inspection stations along the Silk Road to make sure that no one smuggled out their secrets to weaving silk.

One legend tells how a wily king of the Chinese city of Khotan persuaded his bride, a Chinese princess, to hide silkworms in her hair. The guards dared not inspect the bride's hair and the secret to making silk escaped. Another story claims that in the 6th century two monks carried silkworms out of China in hollow sticks.

The Parthians realized that there was money to be made from trading silk. They sent trade missions towards the east. The Romans also sent their own merchants out to explore the route and to try to obtain silk at a lower price than that set by the Parthians. For this reason, the trade route to the East was called the Silk Road by the Romans.

With so many valuable goods making their ways east and west, bandits were drawn to the Silk Road. Indeed, the slow-moving caravans were easy targets for a few armed men with swift horses. Danger lurked around the curves of every mountain, in every desert oasis, along the banks of every river. And so the merchants were forced to hire armed guards to protect their caravans. Eventually, walls and forts were built along the Silk Road to add further protection for the merchants. It is believed that sections of the Great Wall of China were built to protect Silk Road merchants from bandits.

Still, very few merchants traveled the full length of the road; most simply covered part of the journey, selling their goods close to home and then returning with their profits. Other merchants would then resell

This detail from an Italian map shows a caravan traveling the Silk Road to China.

the goods to the other merchants, and so on and so on until the goods found their final markets.

The Polos were not like other merchants. They intended to travel virtually the entire length of the Silk Road.

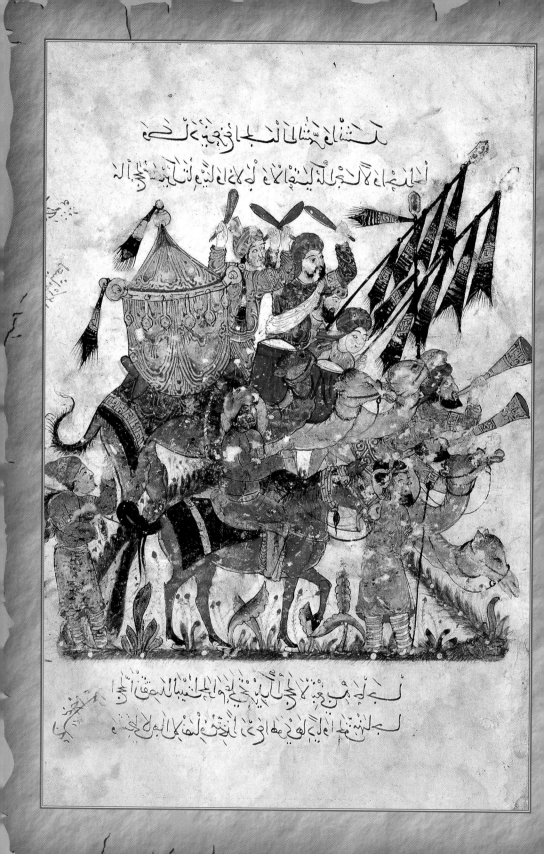

The
Silk Road　　3

The trip to Cathay would take Marco, Maffeo, and Niccolò across deserts, including the vast and scorching Gobi in Mongolia. In Central Asia, they would climb tall mountains and march through deep snow. The three Venetians would travel by horse, camel, and yak. They would sail up rivers aboard oar-powered galleys. Sometimes, they would walk.

The Polos were often delayed by heavy rains that turned the roads into mud. In the deserts, strong winds would whip up blinding sandstorms. In the mountains, a sudden avalanche could close the road and they would have to find a path around the tons of rock. This might take the Polos miles out of their way. And they always had to be on the lookout for bandits.

Through it all, young Marco took notes. In Armenia, Marco laid eyes on Mount Ararat, where Noah's Ark supposedly came to a rest after the Great Flood that is reported in the Bible. Marco found himself more interested in the terrain around the mountain than in its biblical significance. He noted that Mount Ararat's lower slopes had plenty of water and provided for excellent grazing for cattle and sheep. In Georgia, a mountainous region near Russia, Marco noticed that the area was rich in oil. "It is a substance spurting from the ground and used for burning in lamps," he wrote.

Elsewhere, he found "a remarkable material which can be spun into thread and woven into cloth that will not burn when thrust into the fire." The material was asbestos.

He had his first taste of a coconut on the journey: "It is a nut the size of a man's head, pleasant to taste and white as milk."

On seeing his first crocodile, Marco described it as a "huge serpent, ten paces in length, with jaws wide enough to swallow a man."

In the Middle East, the caravan stopped for a time in Hormuz. In Marco Polo's day, Hormuz was an important port city. The Polos had hoped to find a boat in Hormuz to take their caravan across the Persian Gulf.

"Merchants come here by ship from India," Marco wrote, "bringing all sorts of spices and precious stones and pearls and cloths of silk and gold and elephants' tusks and many other wares."

Marco noticed that the people of Hormuz lived mostly on salted fish, onions, and a type of fruit from a palm tree called a *date*. "The natives do not eat our sort of food," he wrote, "because a diet of wheaten bread and meat would make them ill."

The Polos eventually decided to continue on foot. They had concluded that the ships they saw in the Hormuz harbor were not very safe. "Their ships are very bad," wrote Marco. "They are not fastened with iron nails but stitched together with a thread made of coconut husks."

The caravan turned north toward Persia. During the journey across the Persian desert, the Polos met up with the Karuanas, a half-Indian, half-Mongol people who lived as bandits and were greatly feared by travelers. Marco wrote that the Karuanas were said to have mastered "magical and diabolical arts, by means of which they are enabled to produce darkness, obscuring the light of day to such a degree that persons are invisible to one another." Perhaps the Karuanas were simply taking advantage of the fog that would often settle over the desert. Marco never recorded in his notes whether he actually believed in the stories. Nevertheless, the Polos found themselves under attack by a Karuana raiding party. They hid in a nearby tower and eventually escaped, although some members of their caravan were captured and others were killed.

Along the way, the expedition also lost the two monks Pope Gregory had sent with the caravan. Friar Nicholas and Friar William had grown more and more nervous about the bandit attacks on the caravan. One day, the two monks turned back and returned to Italy.

After leaving Persia, the caravan entered Badakhshan, a cold, mountainous region that is now a part of Afghanistan. Marco believed that the Muslim people he met here were descended from Alexander the Great, the Greek conqueror who had explored Asia and the Middle East around 330 B.C. Marco found that the people of Badakhshan were

This illustration from an Arabian book published in 1240 shows a caravan resting at an oasis. Marco Polo's caravan made a longer stop in Badakhshan to wait for him when he became very sick around 1274.

masters of horsemanship. In his notebook, he wrote his suspicion that their strong and swift horses were descended from one of Alexander's warhorses.

In Badakhshan, Marco became very sick. The Polos were delayed for a year while he recovered.

When Marco was strong enough, the caravan pushed on, making its way through the Pamir Mountains. Here, the Polos met Kirghiz herdsmen, who told Marco that he had set foot on the "Roof of the World."

"No birds fly here because of the height and the cold," wrote Marco. "And I assure you that, because of this great cold, fire is not so bright here nor of the same color as elsewhere, and food does not cook well." A hot fire requires oxygen; in higher altitudes, there is less oxygen in the air, so the Polos' cooking fires lacked the fuel they needed to burn.

It took the caravan 52 days to cross the Pamir Mountains. As the Polos finally descended from the Pamirs, they found themselves on a great plain in Western China. They stopped in such cities as Kashgar, Yarkland, and Khotan. Marco made careful notes of what he found in each city: Kashgar produced cotton cloth; Yarkland featured expert craftsmen, and Khotan had many farms, vineyards, and gardens. From Khotan,

Today, the sheep of the Pamir Mountains are named after Marco Polo. In Latin, the Pamir sheep are known as *Ovis poli.* (*Ovis* is the Latin word for "sheep.")

the Polos faced one more stretch of rough travel before they reached the palace of Kublai Khan: the vast and scorching Gobi Desert.

First, they rested in the city of Lop, at the edge of the Gobi, where they let their tired horses rest and eat the tall desert grass. From there, they set out across the Gobi for the long desert crossing. Each day, the party could walk to the next *oasis*, a green and fertile area where water could be found. But there was no food, so they were forced to pack plenty of *provisions* before they left.

By day, the Gobi desert was hot and arid. The scorching sun beat down on the caravan. The Polos had to endure daytime temperatures well over 100 degrees Fahrenheit and terrible sandstorms. At night, the temperatures dipped; even around their campfires, the men shivered under their blankets. What's more, at night the desert was an eerie place, the dark moonless sky black and often frightening.

"When a man is riding by night through this desert and something happens to make him loiter and lose touch with his companions, by dropping asleep or for some other reason, and afterwards he wants to rejoin them, then he hears spirits talking in such a way that they seem to be his companions,"

It took Marco and his companions a month to cross t

Marco wrote in his book. "Sometimes, indeed, they even hail him by name. Often, these voices make him stray from the path, so that he never finds it again. And in this way, many travelers have been lost and have perished."

ormous Gobi Desert, with its shifting sands.

For years, the Chinese called the Gobi the "Flow-
ing Sands" because the fierce Gobi wind constantly
rearranged the positions of the desert's sand dunes.
Travelers would claim to be able to hear the sounds
of the shifting sands. They said this "whispering" of

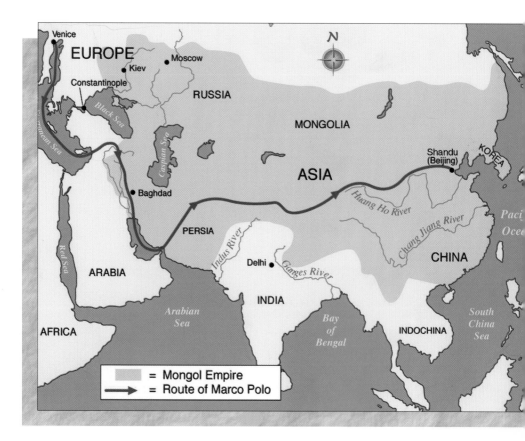

This map shows the route that Niccolò, Maffeo, and Marco Polo took to reach Kublai Khan's palace in Shandu. Their trip across Asia took nearly four years.

the sands was actually the voice of a spirit calling out to the traveler.

"Do not stray from your caravan," the Polos were told by an experienced desert traveler while they rested at an oasis, "for it is then that the spirits do their evil work. They will call out your names as though they are your friends calling to you, and following their voices you will be led in the wrong direction and hopelessly lost."

The Polos trudged on. Finally, they reached the end of the Gobi. It had taken them 30 days to cross this vast desert of shifting sands. Soon, they arrived in Shandu. They were met by an escort sent out to meet them by the emperor. They were to be led to an audience with the great Khan.

It was 1275. The Polos had been on the road for nearly four years. They had endured the hardships of the deserts, the mountains, and the jungles. They had escaped from bandits and overcome sickness. Their journey had covered 12,000 miles. And now, finally, they would meet Kublai Khan.

In the
Palace of
Kublai Khan

Niccolò, Maffeo, and Marco Polo meet Kublai Khan, the powerful ruler of the Mongol Empire. The Khan took a special liking to the teenage Marco Polo.

4

arco, his father and uncle were led to the palace of Kublai Khan. They immediately bowed to show respect for the great leader. The Khan ordered them to rise and expressed his great joy at seeing the brothers again. Then, the Khan saw Marco, who was by then 21 years old. He asked who this young man was.

"Your majesty, this is my son and your servant," replied Niccolò.

The great Khan replied: "He is welcome and it pleases me much."

At this point, the Polos took the opportunity to look around and observe the Khan's magnificent palace. The palace was located inside a fortified inner city within Shandu. The walls of the palace were decorated with carved dragons and paintings of birds, animals and war scenes. The roof shone in the sunshine with its spectrum of colors: yellow, red, blue, green, and violet. Not far from the palace was a hill where Kublai Khan ordered the most beautiful trees from all over the world to be planted.

> Marco Polo described Kublai Khan in this way: "He is a man of good stature, neither short nor tall but of moderate height. . . . His complexion is fair and ruddy like a rose, the eyes black and handsome, the nose shapely and set squarely in place.

"The Khan loves these trees," a guide told the Polos. "Whenever he hears of an unusually rare specimen he orders that it should be carefully dug up and planted here."

On the top of the hill, called Green Mount, there was a magnificent *pavilion* where the emperor would worship. At the foot of the Green Mount, the Polos found a big lake in which all manner of fish were swimming, intended for the Khan's table. Kublai Khan's four wives lived inside the palace. Ten thousand guards watched over the palace. Behind the Green Mount were the Khan's stables, with stalls for his 1,000 white horses.

Near the Khan's palace the Polos found a small but magnificent palace. The Khan's oldest son, Chinkin, lived here. Chinkin would one day become ruler of the Mongol Empire. Kublai Khan had 21 other sons, and four wives.

Kublai Khan staged huge banquets in large halls near the palace. His servants served enough food for 6,000 people. The emperor would sit on an elevated pedestal. Beside him, on an enormous table, was a big jar made of pure gold and filled with wine. As the Khan brought the wine to his lips, musicians would play and everybody would kneel until the emperor had finished his drink. When the banquet was finished, entertainers and dancers would amuse the guests until dawn.

Every year on Sept. 28–the emperor's birthday– 20,000 noblemen would arrive at the palace, all wearing golden robes decorated with jewels and pearls of enormous value. Another large celebration was held on the New Year, when Kublai Khan was presented with gifts of gold, silver, precious stones, and beautiful horses. As many as 5,000 elephants would parade in Shandu. After the parade, the noblemen would gather in a great hall. "Bow down and worship!" would be ordered, and everybody had to bow until his forehead touched the floor. Then they would treat themselves to food and drink.

The Khan was shown great respect. People in his company had to lower their voices and behave humbly. Visitors had to take off their shoes before entering his palace.

Marco observed how bath water was heated. The Khan's servants would use a large quantity of fuel in the form of "black stones." These stones would burn from evening until the next morning. As he watched the stones burn, Marco realized that the Chinese had discovered a use for coal.

Outside the palace, Shandu was a vibrant and densely populated city. Roads led from Shandu to all the corners of Cathay.

The Khan employed messengers on horseback who could bring him news from the most distant parts of his huge empire in a few days. The Khan

When Marco Polo arrived in Shandu, he found Kublai Khan's city to be more splendid than any city in Europe. More than 100,000 people lived in Shandu. At the center of the city was a park where the emperor lived.

had also set up a post office run by messengers. They would carry small packages on horseback from place to place along a system of roads. Every horseman would be given permission to pass in the form of a small plaque. This pass indicated where the rider came from and in which direction he was going. When the rider reached one station he would show his plaque and take another, which would give him permission to ride to the next station. Marco Polo estimated that there were at least 10,000 stations in Cathay and at least 300,000 riders.

Marco Polo found that Kublai Khan wanted his subjects to live a decent life. If storms or swarms of insects ruined their harvests, he would give them food and not ask them to pay taxes. If a family was hit by a disaster, the members would be given as much food and clothes as they had the previous year. Children without a family were brought up in special institutions, and many hospitals were built.

Of course, the Khan had an interest in seeing that his people were well taken care of. After all, if they were hungry or poor or their crops failed, they would not be able to pay their taxes. He knew it was best to help the needy, knowing that one day they would be ready to return the favor by becoming hard workers.

One of Kublai Khan's great accomplishments was building the Great Canal. This waterway stretched 1,000 miles from Shandu to Hangchou. The canal made it easier to travel from the capital to the southern part of China.

The emperor encouraged education and learning. He established schools, and promoted the study of **astronomy** and **geography**. To keep his empire a nice place to live, Kublai Khan also planted trees along both sides of every big road.

Kublai Khan was also very interested in religion. He was greatly disappointed when he learned the two monks dispatched by Pope Gregory had turned back. Still, he asked to see the Polos' copy of the Bible, and told them that he observed the holidays of four major religious groups: Christians, Muslims, Jews, and Buddhists.

"I respect and honor all four great prophets: Jesus Christ, Mohammed, Moses, and Buddha, so that I can appeal to any one of them in heaven," explained Kublai Khan.

Master
Marco Polo

In his travels on behalf of Kublai Khan, Marco Polo visited many strange and exotic places. Among them was India, which he described in great detail in his book.

5

K ublai Khan quickly grew fond of young Marco Polo. "If this youth lives to manhood, he cannot fail to prove himself a man of sound judgment and true worth," the emperor said. From that point on, Marco Polo enjoyed the Khan's great favor and affection. The Khan ordered that the people of Cathay must address him by the title "Master" Marco Polo. Kublai Khan also decided to send Marco on many adventures across Cathay.

In the service of the Khan, Marco Polo would visit Burma, Korea, Tibet, and India. Wherever Marco arrived he found prosperous communities.

As Marco visited the far corners of the Khan's realm, he discovered that many cities used paper money. Kublai Khan had introduced the use of **banknotes** to his kingdom. He had banknotes made of thick paper that was produced by pounding the bark of mulberry trees. The paper was cut to the desired size and stamped in the palace with special colors. The paper money could be exchanged at any time for gold of equal value.

Marco Polo arrived in Burma as the official envoy of Kublai Khan in 1278, one year after a battle had taken place between the king of Burma and the Mongol army of the Khan. On the plain of Vochan, the Mongols had approached with 12,000 well-equipped horsemen to face a Burmese army of 60,000 horsemen and foot soldiers and 2,000 elephants. When the Mongol soldiers saw the elephants they were so scared they wanted to turn back. But the Mongol captain made the horsemen dismount and tie their horses to trees in a nearby wood. His soldiers then started to shoot at the elephants, hitting them with arrows. The frightened elephants stampeded into the woods, crushing the Burmese warriors. When the Mongols saw the stampede, they mounted their horses to chase down the survivors. A fierce battle occurred, and the Mongols defeated the soldiers of Burma.

After the battle the Mongol captain took some elephants to Kublai Khan. From that time on, the emperor always included them in his armies. Unlike the Burmese king, Kublai Khan knew how to use the elephants.

Next, Marco Polo traveled to Manzi, a *province* in southeast Cathay that he would later describe as the richest area of the empire. The local rulers of Manzi did not want to be ruled by the Khan. Immediately after Marco's arrival, the Khan's army crushed the Manzi resistance, forcing the rulers to recognize the Mongol reign. Marco wrote that the queen only stopped fighting when she heard that the Mongol's army commander was called "Hundred Eyes." Fortune tellers in Manzi had predicted that a man with 100 eyes would conquer the kingdom.

After leaving Manzi, Marco was sent by the Khan to serve as governor of Yangzhou. This city was an important shipping port along the Khan's Great Canal. Kublai Khan was suspicious of the local officials, believing that they stole from the city's treasury. So he ordered them arrested and appointed Marco to head the government of Yangzhou. He remained there for three years.

While Marco, his father, and his uncle were in Cathay, they did more than just learn the ways of the people. They also brought some of their culture to the Khan's empire. For three years, the Mongol army laid *siege* to the rich silk town of Xiangyang but failed to capture it because it was encircled by *moats*–ditches filled with water. The Mongol horsemen could not rush the city because their horses could not jump over the moats. Kublai Khan himself traveled to Xiangyang to see the moats. The Khan ordered his military leaders to find a solution.

Marco Polo, already an experienced diplomat, arrived at Xiangyang with Niccolò and Maffeo. Marco told Kublai Khan that he would help him to capture the city by building catapults. The large machines "will throw such big stones that the station will not be able to withstand the siege," Marco told the Khan.

The Polos supervised construction, and they asked the two merchants who had accompanied them to Cathay to help. The traders were a German

The medieval catapult could fire rocks or other projectiles at enemy fortifications.

and a man from the Middle East, and both had built catapults before. After much work, three catapults were finished. When the emperor saw the machines launch the stones, he was delighted. He ordered the catapults brought to the moats of Xiangyang.

When the catapults were ready, one big stone was shot from each weapon into the town. The stones destroyed several buildings and caused panic among the people. The frightened town leaders surrendered to Kublai Khan.

Next, Marco Polo traveled to India. He found that the Indians could weave cotton, and that they held great reverence for oxen and refused to eat them. He also reported that the Indians liked to chew leaves of betel mixed with lime—a practice that is still popular throughout much of Asia.

In southern India, he found divers who would search the sea floor for oysters. These divers could hold their breath for incredible lengths of time. When they surfaced and opened the oysters, they often found valuable pearls inside. Nearby, on the island of Ceylon, Marco found "more beautiful and valuable rubies than are found in any part of the world, and likewise sapphires, topazes and many other precious stones."

Workers in India pick tea, one of the valuable spices that would drive Portuguese and Spanish voyages of exploration in the 15th and 16th centuries. This picture is from a medieval French edition of Marco Polo's book.

Under the rule of Kublai Khan, the Mongol empire grew to include all of present-day China, Mongolia, Korea, Afghanistan, Iran, and Iraq, as well as parts of Siberia, Russia, Turkey, Syria, Pakistan, and India. The kings of Vietnam, Cambodia, and India paid **tribute** to the Khan, meaning their lands fell under his protection. For 17 years, the Polos traveled across the Khan's realm.

"Our Parting
Will Be
Difficult"

Niccolò, Maffeo, and Marco Polo are shown at the far left of the second row in this Italian painting. After living in the Mongol Empire for nearly 20 years, the Polos returned to Venice in 1295.

6

he Khan was now 76 years old—an incredible age for a man during a time when there were few good cures for diseases. Marco, Maffeo, and Niccolò were worried. If the Khan died, they were afraid that jealous **rivals** at court would make things difficult for the three favored foreigners. Also, they were homesick for Venice. After all, they had been away for 22 years. They asked the Khan if they could return home.

The Khan did not want to lose his friends. At first he refused to allow them to leave. Eventually, however, he changed his mind. When the Khan learned that the queen of Persia had died, he decided to send the king of Persia a new queen. So he selected a woman from his court named Kokachin, then summoned the Polos. He asked them to guide her to Persia. Once they had fulfilled this duty, they would be free to travel home to Venice.

"As you can see, I am now an old man, 76 years of age," Kublai Khan told Marco. "And I know it will not be many more years before I join my honorable ancestors. I have been thinking of this in recent times and I have also thought of you and your father and uncle. And although I am greatly attached to all of you and our parting will be very difficult, I feel I have no right to hold you any longer. We have all been good friends and we have been very fortunate to have had so many happy years together. But now we must part. You have all served me faithfully through the years and you will serve me once more by escorting Lady Kokachin to Persia."

The Khan prepared 13 ships for the Polos. They sailed off through the Yellow Sea, then through the **strait** (narrow sea passage) that separates Taiwan from the mainland. Next, the Polos journeyed across the China Sea, through the Bay of Bengal and the Indian Ocean, and finally into the Arabian Sea and the Persian Gulf. Lady Kokachin made the journey safely and was presented to the king.

The sea journey to Persia had taken 30 months. The Polos decided to rest in Persia for a short time. They stayed in Persia for nine months. When they heard that Kublai Khan had died, the Polos decided it was time to leave for Venice.

Kublai's son and *successor*, Chinkin Khan, was far less interested in European culture than his father had been. Soon, peaceful trade between East and West would end. Within 100 years, the Mongol Empire would collapse. Traders would no longer be free to travel the Silk Road far into Asia. Indeed, China was on its way to becoming a closed and mysterious corner of the earth.

From Persia, the Polos traveled to Trebizond in eastern Turkey. In Trebizond, they were no longer in the realm of the Khan, so Kublai's protective gold tablets no longer worked. Soon after setting foot in Trebizond, the Polos were robbed by bandits.

From Trebizond, the Polos went to Constantinople. From there, it was a simple matter to book passage on a ship to Venice. They arrived home in 1295. The Polos had been away for 24 years.

The Polos hardly recognized Venice. Indeed, the city had changed while they were gone. New streets had been built and new buildings erected. As for the Polos themselves, they had, of course, aged. Marco had been a 17-year-old boy when the caravan set out for Cathay. Now, he was 41 years old—a man of middle age. Also, the trip home had been difficult and the three men were dressed in rags.

The men knocked on the door of the Polo home. A servant answered but did not recognize the men. They told him they were the Polos—Niccolò, Maffeo, and Marco. The servant did not believe them, so he summoned members of the family. No one recognized the Polos. They were taken for beggars and asked to leave. At that point, Niccolò, Maffeo, and Marco ripped open the seams of their filthy clothes, and out poured streams of rubies, diamonds, and emeralds. The Polos had sewn the precious jewels inside their clothes so that they would not be stolen on the journey.

The family staged a lavish banquet to welcome home the travelers. When Marco was asked about his travels, he spoke about the wonders he had seen.

Marco Polo's book was the first best-seller. It was very popular, and the story was translated into many languages. For over 700 years, people have enjoyed reading The Book of Marco Polo.

Marco would not get a chance to say much else about his journey until he found himself sharing a jail cell with Rustichello. For in the Polos' absence, Genoa and Venice had slowly grown to be bitter enemies, and in 1295 war was brewing between the two city-states. In a few months, Marco would be commanding a galley in the Venetian navy. And then came the battle off the coast of Curzola Island, and his capture and imprisonment.

After a year, peace was established between the city-states. Marco was released from prison, and returned home to Venice. His aging father and uncle soon died. Marco became a man of great wealth. He married and soon had a family of three daughters.

But although Marco's book was published in many languages, the story of his journey was not believed. People regarded his observations as lies. They could not believe that the Khan had been so rich and powerful and had commanded an army that conquered virtually all of Asia. And the stories of what Marco had found on his journey—from the crocodiles and coconuts, to the use of coal, to the paper money, to the descriptions of the incredible mountains and vast deserts of Central Asia—well, it was just too much to comprehend.

Marco Polo lived to be 70 years old. On January 9, 1324, he lay in bed dying. He was surrounded by friends and members of the clergy who urged him to admit that he had made up his stories.

"Confess all!" people urged him. "Confess that it has been a hoax. Confess that it is all untrue before the breath leaves your body and it is too late."

With his last breath, Marco told them: "I have not told half of what I saw."

Chronology

1211 Genghis Khan leads his Mongol army across Central Asia and Europe and establishes the Mongol Empire.

1254 Marco Polo is born in Venice, Italy.

1259 Kublai Khan, grandson of Genghis Khan, becomes ruler of the Mongol Empire

1269 Niccolò and Maffeo Polo return from their first trip to Cathay, where they have befriended Kublai Khan.

1271 Niccolò, Marco and Maffeo Polo set out for what would become a 24-year trip across the empire of Kublai Khan.

1275 The Polos arrive in Shandu, the Khan's summer palace.

1292 The Polos leave Cathay and return to Venice.

1294 Kublai Khan dies.

1295 The Polos arrive home in Venice.

1296 Marco Polo is captured during the war between Venice and Genoa. He spends a year in prison, where he dictates the story of his adventures to Rustichello, a writer from Pisa, Italy.

1324 Marco Polo dies on January 9.

Glossary

armada–a fleet of warships.

astronomy–the study of objects and matter that are outside the earth's atmosphere, such as the stars and planets. Because sailors used the stars to guide their journeys, an understanding of astronomy was important for navigation.

banknote–a written promise issued by a bank or by the government that can be used as money. (for example, a dollar bill is a banknote issued by the government).

caravan–a company of travelers on a journey through desert or hostile regions. People traveled in caravans to protect themselves from bandits and brigands.

city-state–an independent state consisting of a city and the surrounding territory.

date–the oblong, edible fruit of a certain kind of palm tree.

emissary–a person sent on a mission on behalf of a leader; official messenger.

galley–a long,, low type of ship that was powered primarily by oars and used for war and trading on the Mediterranean Sea.

geography–the study of the earth's form, and its division into land and sea areas.

moat–a deep, wide trench, usually filled with water, that surrounds a fortified city or castle.

oasis–a fertile, green area in an arid desert.

palace–the official home of an emperor, head of state, or ruler of a country.

parchment–a dried animal skin (often sheep or goat) that was used for paper in Medieval times.

pavilion–a light, ornamental building, often located in a garden or park.

province–a region of a country, usually separated from other provinces for geographical or political reasons.

provisions–a stock of food and water.

prowess–extraordinary ability or skill.

rival–two persons who compete with each other to achieve the same goals.

silk–a lustrous, fine, and elastic fiber produced by silkworms and woven into fabric.

Silk Road–a network of roads and trails that linked Europe with the countries of the Far East in the 13th century.

spices–any of various aromatic vegetable products, such as pepper or nutmeg, used to season or flavor foods. In the 15th and 16th centuries, spices were rare and highly valued by the people of Europe.

strait–a relatively narrow passageway that connects two large bodies of water.

successor–a person who gains a title or power, usually with the support of the previous ruler.

Further Reading

Dramer, Kim. *Kublai Khan*. New York: Chelsea House
  Publishers, 1990.

Komroff, Manuel. *Marco Polo*. New York: Simon and Schuster,
  1952.

Larner, John. *Marco Polo and the Discovery of the World*. New
  Haven: Yale University Press, 1999

MacDonald, Fiona. *Marco Polo: A Journey Through China*.
  Danbury, CT: Franklin Watts, 1998

Polo, Marco. *The Travels of Marco Polo*. Edited by Ronald
  Letham. New York: Viking, 1982.

Stefoff. Rebecca. *Marco Polo and the Medieval Explorers*. New
  York: Chelsea House Publishers, 1992.

Wood, Frances. *Did Marco Polo Go To China?* Boulder, CO:
  Westview Press, 1998.

Picture Credits

HAL MARCOVITZ is a journalist for the *Allentown Morning Call* in Pennsylvania. In 1993 and 1996, his columns were awarded the Keystone Press Award by the Pennsylvania Newspaper Publishers Association. His first book was the satirical novel *Painting the White House.* He has also written a biography of Francisco Coronado for Chelsea House's EXPLORERS OF NEW WORLDS series. He lives in Chalfont, Pennsylvania, with his wife, Gail, and daughters Michelle and Ashley.